H
W
BUTTERFLY

Loic Ekinga

Published by Ensorcellia,
an imprint of Odyssey Books, in 2021

www.odysseybooks.com.au

A Cataloguing-in-Publication entry is available from
the National Library of Australia

ISBN: 978-1922311306 (pbk)
ISBN: 978-1922311313 (ebook)

HOW TO
WAKE A
BUTTERFLY

"Once upon a time, I dreamt I was a butterfly, fluttering hither and thither, to all intents and purposes a butterfly. I was conscious only of my happiness as a butterfly, unaware that I was myself. Soon I awaked, and there I was, veritably myself again. Now I do not know whether I was then a man dreaming I was a butterfly, or whether I am now a butterfly, dreaming I am a man."

— *Zhuangzi*

Caterpillar

I had to believe that it ends easier than it begins, eventually.

How it almost began

Has the little boy told you
About the first time his life was saved?
It's a short story, really.
It involves
Sharp tools, a man, a little girl
And a doctor with a conscience.

How it began

She hums to a gospel song/the doctor asks her mother and sister to get her to talk/is there anything eating her/she needs to let go of hurt to ensure a safe delivery/the baby (you) is cut out of her/she did speak to someone/you were not an easy pregnancy/it's a boy/it's a problem/it's a screaming caterpillar/it won't even look like its father/there was blood /a lot of it/there was always blood/she hums some more/will the baby grow wings/he has known so much hurt already.

Bana ya Espe

Bana' a Espe,
Espe's children
Was their collective name.
Carl, the boy with leopard skin
And smooth sideburns
Always tucking his mother's
Dress, wanting to exist;
Hénoc the light-skinned, skinny-necked,
Big-eyed baby who existed
With no need for tucking, no nagging
As if existing was owed to him
And it was.
And the little, big boy with his rabbit teeth
Being reminded to take on responsibilities
In order to exist.
For the three of them, it's been twenty years
And nothing much has changed.

Mutilate

The year is 2001
My mother looks down at me
And tells me that she's going away to study.
She's taking my baby brother with her
I should've asked her why was home
Not good enough a classroom but I didn't
And I let her walk because she promised
To explain everything one day, soon.
Later that evening and many evenings
After that, I watched my father
Attempt to climb Mount Sinai
Hoping to catch a glimpse of God's back.
My dad filled every room in the house
With the silence he exhaled,
A silence my brother and I inhaled
The same silence that spread like
A virus under our skin
We grew into hollow men
My brother and I.
20 years later, we're having this conversation
Again,
This time, she's in Chicago not here still

I sit on the dirty blue rug of the room
I'm renting and she's worried about my sanity
While I'm trying to hold her hand through the phone.
"You've found so much comfort
Away from home, on the road
I don't understand, why."
And in a way, only she masters,
My mother spoke to the ten-year-old me
Like rain speaks to dust
And quietens dirt.
"I've found no comfort, son.
I left for you, because sometimes,
To save the hand, you cut off a finger."

My father: a quick lesson in silence

My father taught me
To be a wielder of silence
A master of body language.
He taught me that questions
Don't always guarantee answers
That sometimes, if you're silent
Enough, the answer will come knocking.
In 2001, when my mother left,
I didn't know what it all meant
And my father carried on as he did
Everyday:
News, food, bed.
And somewhere in between
He would call us to gather and pray.
My father cried when he prayed
In fact, my brothers and I used to mock
Him in our room.
We were too young to understand that
Form of therapy.
My father taught me to be a wielder
Of silence, it's better than flinging
Sounds across the room out of anger,

And even more embarrassingly,
Hurt.
It's been fifteen years since I last saw him
And I still don't know what questions to ask.
Lately, I've been unlearning silence,
I've been scraping off my bones the glue
That comes with sighs
This life is getting too loud
This life wants me to answer
And I've been nervous about losing
The only thing that makes me my
Father's son.

Adrien, back home; in the mud

A little boy with rabbit teeth
And large lips meets another boy,
Adrien, with his large ears – instant attraction,
Instant association.
Adrien can make a toy out of anything
So he fashions worlds and stories
Out of sticks and mud from
The trees and golden sands
In the boy's grandmother's garden.

~

The little boy has a beard now,
His teeth are straight and his lips
Are referred to as "full" now.
But on rare days when he doesn't worry
About bills or a future or love fleeting
He remembers the kaleidoscope
Of white butterflies
That seemed to emerge from the gold
Of the earth and Adrien running after them.
On those days,
The little boy aches to go back to the mud.

On my parents' divorce

I believed in God
At 10, when I didn't have to ...
(Children don't need to believe
In Christ to make it to heaven)
I was told, God listens to little boys'
Prayers
Yet I felt my heart sink and dry
On my pillow at night
Like my parents' marriage,
In Jesus' name. Amen

Pressed down, shaken together

The boy is pressed. It's 2am
The bathroom is locked
The boy knocks on his cousin's door softly
The boy is afraid to wake the man
Of the house.

So he bends and pees in his backpack
Pocket.
In the morning, the family questions
The boy's Christianity and spiritual state
From then on, boy
It's the devil in you, all the time.

Up the mountain, down the valley

The boy is lying prostrate
Weakened by a 5-day fast
The prophet lashes at him
In tongues
So
The boy spreads himself wide
To receive.
What theft! What treachery!
It is said that God allowed Moses
To see His back on Mount Sinai
The boy knows now, like Moses
What it feels like to plead to a God
Who's walking away.

My father:
a lesson in mourning like a man

The first time I saw the little
Boy inside my dad
Was the day we found out
That Koko Mwasi passed
My dad traipsing out of his
Room with black shades on
And a manhood he wore like
A necklace
Or that hand that grabs a man's throat
To support his chin.
He walked in one way
And my brothers and I felt oxygen leave the room
The other way.
"Ça va?" his ex-wife would ask
And with a voice that has just fallen
Off a bicycle, my dad croaked
Half smiling, half dying.
His grief at the time must have felt like a bag of
Marbles in his stomach
And I asked myself
Why aren't you crying?
What is this?

Why are you hiding?
Why are you hiding?
Should I not cry too?
If this is what it means to be a man
Then I'd rather be porous.

My father: a lesson in archiving

Carl, my brother, is on the phone
With Dad
And I recklessly drag my feet into the room
Saying something
"Is that Loic talking in the back?"
"I'm here, Dad"
And he is shocked at the bass in my voice
This is what 15 years does
Unfamiliarity
At night, I need to keep the lights off
To remind myself what time it is
It's time to sleep, boy
You have school tomorrow
And I snore like he did 15 years ago
I hear my bloodline against my pillow
Like crashing waves and
Hysterical laughter, the men that came
Before me were all triers and I sometimes
Think that I need to try to not be those men
That I am more than a seed from a rotten
Fruit on the side of the road
Dropped by a traveller in a hurry

To someday meet and marvel at the bass
He installed in my throat with a kiss
I am story that wrote itself
I am pages stained with ink and Ds
Shaped like Bs and Ls
Like my First Grade exercise book
At 5 I learned how to read, and my father
Marvelled at my love for words
But he didn't know that
I was a little boy who needed to read
What was on the 7 o'clock news
He liked the news, maybe then we'd have
Something to talk about
I ask what "archives" means
He says old things that are kept
To be looked at again
The day Koko Mwasi passed
And I watched him cover his grief
Behind a pair of Ray-Bans
I wondered if this is ever gonna be
An archive
We will look at again.
Dad, stories like ours write themselves
Stories like ours cannot be archived

Origin story

Sometimes, I imagine the first time
my parents met.
I imagine Madilu System filling
a warm November night
with another song about a longing man
and an indifferent woman.
I see my dad, still young
back when he was sure about himself
whispering in my mother's ear about
rainy days in bed

                                        CUT TO:

My mom in her bunk bed, asleep
to the sound of butterflies and buzzers
visiting the flowerbed inside her chest.
I imagine that night and wonder
whether her heart smiled at the hope
of a love that might not leave marks

                                        CUT TO:

A first kiss. And me
fighting off uncertainty
to come into a world
of peace and so much chaos.

Christening

As soon as I was born,
my mother handed me to Jesus
and made sure I was presentable.
As soon as I could talk
she told me about salvation
about how to avoid hell
and be good.
There was always so much fire
I didn't know back then that I was born
a sinner
I didn't know back then that sometimes
instilling fear is sort of a love language.

Growing up, there

The first time I saw a grown man's penis
was when Ya Makiadi ran in a frenzy
towards my grandmother's house
it was said that the witches
in our neighbourhood were jealous
of the falsetto that shot out of his throat
on Sunday mornings
"how does the devil sit in church?"
someone always asked
the answer, I remember, was something
about Job and a gathering in heaven
maybe the devil belongs here
and just like on the day Ya Makiada ran screaming
something in a strange language
I'd come to know madness and violence too
like in '97 when the bombs
set the sky ablaze and my brother – still a baby –
hit the floor
or when the big nosed prophet my family
invited to snuff out Satan
reminded us that we had fingers
that could be pointed at each other

cousins and uncles learned how to hug
with the cold blade of machetes kissing
their now bare backs
with the cold blade of mistrust
pressed where reassuring hands should
or even the night I squeezed my head
between my hands, praying for sleep
to take me
as growls and clamouring laughter
from an exorcism bounced off
the living room walls.
I have seen enough to write this poem
I have...

...when the devil ended his stay
on my grandmother's roof
I asked Ya Makiadi what happened on that day
he smiled and as if he thought I didn't already
know
said

"nothing".

Mwana moninga mawa te

When I was a child, I remember playing
soldier with my friends
we used our fingers as guns
and death was always a debate...

la guerre a commencée,
tout le monde en position
mwana moninga mawa te!
The war has begun
everyone take position
no mercy for a friend's child!

Sometimes, among all the violence,
I wish I could go back to a time
I could argue and tell death
"not today, the bullet didn't hit me!"

Cocoon

Dit au monde entier que je suis entrain de m'éteindre

First day in Lubumbashi

Car ride from the airport. The little boy
Sharing the back seat with Carl
Is capturing with his eyes the new landscape.
The earth here isn't golden like his
Grandmother's, it's red
Like fire.
The mountain on the wheel is spitting that fire
Towards the boy's mother who cowers against the
Car door.
The boy is looking out the window
Trying to steady his breathing
Trying to already forget as the smoke
Of unfamiliarity fills the blue Toyota.

Likasi

There was a ten-year age gap between them
A long, long distance
The woman lies on her back, naked
Expecting to feel.
The little boy traces her body with his eyes
From between her thighs all the way to her
Smiling face.
A long, long distance.

Likasi... again

Eh eloko nayo
Munene boye!
Bana baluba
Baliesaka bino nini?*

*if you're confused about what she said
know that the boy was too. Also, know that she
grabbed it quite hard.

Likasi... one more time

In the kitchen that evening
She's spread before the boy
Her right thigh reaching as far as
The freezer
Her cleavage, a crucifix
Atop the hill around her navel
That same night, under bed sheets
And secrets
Someone stopped growing.

Likasi... for the last time

Boy,
Don't blame yourself
For your love of cheap erotic films
(They were French, after all)
And they came to you
Even when you scoured through
The TV channels like a hyena
Hoping to suck on the bones
Of what society has spit out
Don't blame yourself
Even when the lady sucked
On the confused bone between
Your legs
She came to you
(She was available, after all)

Likasi... because I'm trying to get over it

It's extremely wrong to be molested
And claim to be the man in charge
A lucky, lucky boy.

Likasi... I think I'm over it now

Yesterday:
"I'm sure all the girls in your class want you, if only they knew"

Today:
Pornhub search bar: "Milf videos"

Phone conversation with a hint of the old denial

We'll tell each other the truth
From now on, okay?
Cool.
Just don't ask me about my childhood
Yes... yes... I was fifteen, yes...
No, please don't ask
Ugh... yes, the truth
She touched me, I touched her
No need to therapize me
Yes, she was twenty-seven...
No... it wasn't molestation
I'm clearly fine... denial?
Wow... allo?... you were saying
I just prefer older women...
It's not a sexual fantasy! Don't make me laugh
Have I what?...
Allo?... thought of your mum?
While doing what?...
Um...

Rupture

I didn't have to doubt myself like that

Let me start by saying...

I'm sorry for setting your body
On fire, just to worship a flame
Back then, I was looking
For a god anywhere
I still haven't found God, today
But at least, I stopped playing
With matches.

Erin's lament

I'm sorry about the cold you felt
Outside this body,
I'm sorry that I left you on
This table for too long
Like a cup of coffee
By the time I thought of you again,
I couldn't take you in any longer
But look on the bright side,
You're happier, right?
There is a renewed sense of hope
In this house,
I hear chimes on every tree
And batting wings here,
I imagine you wrapped in blankets
Blowing raspberries, thinking of
What to do tomorrow,
I gave you heartbreak and adventure
I too, like you, avoid certain dates
On the calendar
Love songs are dirges now,
Like Erin's Lament, aren't they?
But our bodies ache for other things now,

For other people
I don't know when this grief will
Finally catch up to me,
But for now, I hear chimes on every tree

In fact...

All I needed from you
Was to make me believe
That I could be anything
That I could do anything
That after all is said
And done, I still mattered
That and lots and lots
And lots and lots
And lots and lots
Of hugs

Medicine

One day,
I'll be all water
And medicine
One day, I'll
Slip through your fingers
And you'll lick what's
Left of me on your palm.

Rupture

We don't talk anymore
In this house
Conversations between us
Sprout like mushrooms do:
Out of dead and rotten things
So we avoid words
While our bodies charge at each other
With the fury of a thousand maddened men
Sometimes I wonder if this is what
Love should feel like.

Back back back

Remember when we were
Kids?
When you left me in that cave
On a normal afternoon
It was raining, I remember
You said you'd be right back
You said I shouldn't move
You'd be back...
Then you smiled yourself
Into someone's else's life
You went farther than you promised...
It stopped raining,
May I please leave now?

Jam

One day you'll get
To bite into this fruit
One day my body
Will be liquid in your mouth
And I'll warn you about the worm
Inside my flesh
Because I'm a good guy
But with laughter behind your
Eyes
You will sink your teeth in
So much self doubt and uncertainty
And my skin will turn into jam
Inside your throat

Boy,
Listen more. A woman's tears
Are said to trigger God
Allow yourself to feel
Allow yourself to feel her
How will you see God
When your pockets
Are full of broken versions or yourself.
Now, give her a hug
The last butterfly in her stomach
Needs mouth-to-mouth.

Lunch at Tasha's

We sit at that new restaurant
You've been going on about
For years, back when we were us
I think I know why we're here
Or what I'm doing
You say, "Let's order appetizers"
And I look at you with so much
Silence behind my eyes –
The feelings that rise from my
Stomach and set camp in my mouth
Do things to my breath that
Cigarette smoke would envy –
With so much
Laughter behind your eyes
You add, "When did you become
Such a cheapskate?"
And I want to tell you that for months now,
Life has constantly been spitting at me
But I don't, and order a serving of escargots
I always liked the taste of garlic
And earth, anyway.
"How have you been?"

Me?
I am a 20-something-year-old
Boy who has just rediscovered
His love for crying.
Why? You ask...
Well, because I'm teething
My mouth has been taking
Its first steps, stumbling and stepping
On emotions scattered on the carpet
Like Lego pieces
And you don't seem to notice the swelling,
It baffles me.
No... You see it, you just don't want
To talk about e-v-e-r-y-t-h-i-n-g
There are scabs here, still red,
Ready to ooze loneliness and pain
And cold, cold blood
Men bleed too, a lot actually
Internally, mostly
I want to tell you that I don't want to reconnect,
I really really don't
But I politely sit there and listen to you
Talk about work and escargots
As the sun sets across the distance.

Toys

When you're done playing
With my feelings
Please put your toys away
Don't leave them on the floor
In a mess.

Feels

"You're deeply sensitive man."
I took those words and crushed them.

Inside my palm until they turned
Red like wine, I don't want to cry.
She looked at me again and called me
River.

Just like you

By now, you should know that I know about your
sadness, too. I know about how it crawls into your
bed with its shoes on and takes up most of it, how
it wraps itself under your covers and leaves you
shivering. I, too, have spent many nights to the
thud of the Devil's footsteps on my roof.

I, too, held my breath to make myself invisible.
I know too well the feeling of your sadness gnawing
on the hair at the back of your neck
About avoiding mirrors, and phone calls
and coffee.
I have seen sadness's red eyes and have lost
myself many times in their beauty.
I, too, speak less and less everyday
Smile dismissively and cope by napping.
I couldn't tell you how to get past this
Or when the clouds will start moving again
Or when the hair on your neck will grow again
But I can tell you
What I've learned:

healing hurts.

Dances with the "you know what"

I'm asked,
"When did you become so sensitive?"
What do I say to this?
Have I not outrun this wolf for many years?
Have I not stayed up at night when it stalked
Me through the trees?
I'm at my wit's end, I have hit a brick wall.
I will have to face this beast one way or another.
Let it be today, in my twenties.
There's so much crying I need to catch up
On.

Cry

Tell me,
Why is your heart pacing in your chest?
What is beating the Djembe drum
Inside your mouth, boy?
Have I told you these poems
Are maps to guide you home, my love?
That these words will hurt your feet
Like small shoes would?
Have I? Listen, keep walking
If you need to cry, cry
I won't laugh...
They don't know you like I do
They don't know
That you've been the clown
For a reason.
They don't know that your tears can taste
Like silence too.
Your tears have nothing to say
Your hands are sieves
And your lungs a polluted sky.
If you need to cry, cry
Cry, my love

There's no shame in not
Wanting to get up
Mud builds warm houses too.

Steady, steady now

Boy,
Give yourself a chance
Love with no fear
Live. Today...
This is what you do
When your heart takes
Its first steps:
You hold its hand
Keep it standing,
"Steady, steady now"
Until it flutters by rose petals
And green blades
"Steady, steady for a while now"
Boy,
That one time,
The old man must have been
Right,
Suffering ends, eventually.
This is what you do when
Your heart speaks its first words:
You keep it talking
"Say free for Daddy! Say alive!"

Healing hurts

At this point,
I don't even know
Which parts of me have begun
Rotting
At this point,
The smell could be anything, really
A lie I told, a lie I told myself, manhood
A forced apology, a simple hello
Also,
Parts of me have started a new dialect
I do not understand
And they speak to each other,
Almost shouting
Like neighbours on lands with no streets
I bat my eyelids to look at the future
And they giggle, they mock,
A secret only they know
Tell me, I say
How does it feel to be a man

And to have to cut parts of yourself
To survive
Let your blood be libations
For dead things that laugh and sneer.
For mercy needed
For an awakening that will punch your belly?
Why am I to be my own funeral
And resurrection?

Rapunzel

I'm in a tower with many windows
And no doors
I know what outside looks like
I know the wind is calling me
And if the fall doesn't break me
I will sadly have to welcome
Myself back here, soon

Indistinct chatter

When did your life become
Such a frown?
When did it become a low groan?
A hiccup
An indistinct chatter
When did you become
A sigh?

A plea

I'm afraid that you will
Sigh at my life
Like a firework
That soars across the sky
Never to explode into
A million tiny flames
That you will see
How my skin is a crouching
Figure
How my eyes are big black holes
My existence waving red flags
But I'm trying, I swear!
I wake up every morning, trying.

I want to tell you these things
face to face

Inside my chest,
Is so much noise
Inside my chest, you will hear
Running footsteps and funerals
Wailing and the sound of clinking glass
There's a father that never came close
A child that never left for school
A little boy crying in an unfamiliar
Neighbourhood
There's an uncle telling him to man up
There's a mother that never left a note
A seducing hanging noose
A red pit, a fire pit, Christmas day
And separation
I want to tell you these things, face to face
But how do I tell you these stories
Without you finding yourself in them?
How do I tell you, without offending you
That the shells on the floor, mixed
With my blood
Have your initials engraved on them?
How do I tell you, that I only write

Because I've just learned how to exhale
Without you, wanting to choke me back
To silence?

Winter in a new life

That afternoon, the wind blew cold from
The south
I tied my scarf around my neck,
Almost like a noose
I pulled it a little tighter
Tighter, still
And in that moment,
That very moment, I felt home
Something about thinning air
Makes me feel alive, makes me feel at home.

I am a poplar tree with half browning
Leaves.
Heart-shaped palms with yellow
Hanging fingernails.
If you decide to cut me down,
You will find twenty-nine rings
Like a crackling vinyl pregnant
With songs about things I was too afraid
To say before for the sake of kindness.
Twenty-nine rings of a life with swollen
Feet, a life with a heavy yawn stuck
Inside its bones.

Ya Lolo

Ya Lolo,
Don't push against
Your healing
Are you not the one
Always left last to taste
Your own blood?
Don't push against your healing

When the sky is ready
The sun will rise
Wait for the heat atop a hill
Don't push against your healing, Ya Lolo

~

Don't push against
Your own healing
When the sky is ready
Tomorrow will be at your door
Leave it open
Leave it open and you'll see

A few months before Tasha's

She says
"Let's grow apart together"
She says
"When you leave, wait so I can
Pack my bag too"
I say the door frame is too
Small for us both
That no matter what
I have chaos in my muscles
My bones are heartbreaks
And
I was born with a blood
Ready to run
Ready to splatter on any open path
Ready to stain any passport
She says
"When you leave, please
Take me with you"
And I rode the wind to safety
And never looked down.

This part is for you, Koko Louise

Your love will never leave here

Friday afternoons

1.
Boy,
Friday...
The sun is half asleep
In the turquoise sky
And you have become
A body of a thousand flickering
Lights and laughter.
You go play with your friends
In the streets of Matshotsho
And build little homes with mud
And smiles –
Thicker walls keep the devils at bay
Thicker walls keep heartbreak at bay.

2.
The sun is shutting its eyes
And your grandmother is calling you home
Tomorrow, this will mean something
Foreign, a language full of holes
A bouncing feeling, a void.
It will mean to leave everything behind

To step into ectoplasmic ballrooms
And sway and sway and sway forever
To hold the dress she spent weeks sewing
On the veranda
That patchwork of memories
Of Friday afternoons
Of love that sticks like gum

You miss her, don't you?
I do too.

3.
Sometimes, you're a wet door handle
An instant regret, a starved butterfly
Even as a child,
When you pushed your ear
Against the earth
And it whispered
"Your innocence can only take you so far."
On Friday afternoons you steadied
Your breathing
And walked up
That hill to see her sitting on a stool
Stepping her Singer sewing machine
Into a whirring
Monster of creation.
She will look up from her glasses
And say "bana ya Espe baye"

"Espe's children are here"
And your wings will take shape and colour.

As it turns out, I haven't mourned your passing enough

Before today,
I haven't thought about you
In months.
I really haven't, today I did
And I can't move. I haven't moved
Like grieving you hasn't moved
It's not leaving
It's not leaving
Grandmother
It's not going away!

On family

Funny how
We boomerang into
Each other's lives
With so much anger
And confusion in the stomach
(You will grow and cry here)
We will gather one day
At Grandma's grave
And account for the bleeding
Some will hug, I hope
Others will walk away, I know
(QUIET, BOY! DON'T WRITE ABOUT US!)
Maybe blood is too thick
A liquid to grow a garden

Cycle

it's natural
that you left before me
it's natural
because you landed here decades
ago
and saw the moon before I could be.
but how about
– this is going to sound crazy –
you never left and stayed with me forever,
would you like that?

About tongues

You remember the evening
I asked you what happened
to your tongue?
What happened to you speaking
French to me, everyday?
You said that you forgot how to.
You said it just went away.
Even then, I knew that this is not
how forgetting works.

I'm writing this as proof.

Tu!

You probably know by now
that your grandson
is not a scared little boy anymore
that you don't have to stand outside the toilet
at night,
you don't have to hear me call your name
every time the breeze giggles
to make sure you're there,
keeping the devil at bay.
Koko Louise, you probably
know by now that I look at you still
like I did 25 years ago when I opened the door
and you made that silly sound.

Today, whenever I smell something bad,
I make the same sound
and laugh in disgust
with so much love in my heart.

Butterfly

How do you wake a butterfly?
If you can, I say
–Without bruising its wings–
With a hug

You'd laugh at that

You'd kiss me at last,
And my knees would turn
Liquid

Congregation

I met a girl, once
It was on Instagram.
I was drawn to her words like a butterfly is
To pinks, and yellows
So I left her my number
Smooth move, that.
I met a girl, once
Her skin as radiant as her words
And she spoke with the grace
Of a pearl necklace.
I found out that she'd also lost her grandmother
Sooner than I did mine, but
I imagined them in another life
Getting acquainted before I met the girl.
"My grandson and your granddaughter
Would be perfect for each other"
I imagined my grandmother would say
Then I'd laugh, quietly.
She's a tiny woman from Central Africa
Standing behind a kerosene lamp
And the girl's grandmother a Nubian queen
From the South, humming hymns

Now, pulling strings.
What words do they have in common?
What letters if not the L's in our names...
I met a girl on Instagram, once
I am drawn to her love like a hummingbird
To greens and lilacs
Batting my wings a thousand times over
To stay in one place
To tell her
I'm not going anywhere.
I'm not going anywhere, Honey.

Congregation... still

I imagine heaven
I imagine two women
Sitting across a table with a kerosene
Lamp between them
It's not day nor night.
I imagine
My grandmother sliding an old
Picture of mine across the wooden table
I'm nine, rabbit teeth, skinny arms and ashy knees,
With my fists clenched, smiling
At the photographer, my dad.
The girl's grandmother picks up the picture
Examines it, thoroughly
My grandmother winces, she wants to
Say "you should see what he's grown to look like"
But she can't,
These women don't speak the same language.
The girl's grandmother takes out a picture
Of the girl and holds it next to mine
Holds them to the kerosene lamp.
And after a while
She nods, she smiles

And somewhere between provinces
That night,
Gardens blossomed under our pillows.

Cicada

We hear a flurry of cicadas
Fill the night with ambient sounds
Like footsteps
Like a train station
Or a marketplace
I look at you, carefree
Beside me, humming
To a made up song
You'd say, smiling
"But all songs are made up"
And I would want to tell you
About how much of me
I am about to give you,
You are about to get too much of me.
That same night, I'll watch you sleep,
Ask myself how we happened
And Google alchemy and fate
You'll breathe music into our room
And within the lyrics of breathing
I would find answers.
We happened because we happened
All songs – even beautiful songs –
Are indeed made up.

This woman feels like Sunday

I know a woman
With eyes the colour
Of ebony wood and nights
When the cold throws
Itself against our door
I am a resting man
Who has watched her hold his heart
Against the light
She holds it there, gently
And strokes its colourful wings.
This woman presses her dandelion
Lips against my emotions,
Against my life
I know a woman with a breath
That sounds like the ocean
And days where sun rays peek through
Leaves, where the air smells of flour
And iced tea.
This woman feels like Sundays
This woman feels like Teddy Pendergrass
Peaches and Herb
Salads and swishing mops

Lavender and pot pourri
This woman...
She says come lie down.

And my skin mumbles a song
In a language I'm just starting to understand
And if you decide to travel far enough
And meet her in her fields of yellows
Tell her
That I now understand why I want to live.

Butterflies, starlings, chimes

On one page there's a paragraph
About you, about how you stretch
Your consonants into a symphony
Of measured alliterations
On another, a sentence about my wide
Eyes burning holes into your summer dress
On yet another a drawing made
On a Sunday afternoon
Butterflies, starlings, chimes
In that order
On the cover, hands intertwined
Rising from muscle to skin
Towards the sky, like growing plants
You, smiling the universe into spins
And explosions
You, planting the spine of the earth
Darling, if this love was a book
How many religions
Do you think we would push
Out of our bellies?

At this point, I can't deny it anymore

Here's one more poem about you:
Your smile stretches
Across the provinces between us
And I've loved you in places
My feet haven't touched yet.

I've loved you under sunsets
I haven't seen yet, on sands
I haven't kicked, in words
I haven't written yet
Your smile is a chest
To keep me warm in nights
I have yet to find sleep.

To be quite fair

The truth is, I shouldn't be writing you this many love poems. But everything seems to always come back to you. I imagine that you would, on some Sundays – when I let life press my head against my pillow – call me outside and say something like "The sky is on!" Like you would a TV show, because where there is a sky and darting weaver birds, I should be too. To inhale the day and exhale the present and when my body allows me, to dance too.

The truth is you seem to carry my hurt as well, I think I do. And when there is a need, you lay it down slowly because when boys like me break everyone around needs to have their shoes on. So here I am, ready to give. Ready for everything, you.

Palindrome

Our love is a palindrome
THIS way and that way...
THAT way and this way.

Holding your hand

Someone has mentioned
Your name to God
She does it every evening
Why are you still trying
To grind out your own healing
While dawn is coming to you,
Surely?

Thank you for this

"The sun is always up, here" she says

I need you to know

I will make your body an altar
A place I can return to for worship.

~

By the time we're done
I want to piece together
Your limbs spread across
This bedroom floor
I want to ruin you
And build you up again
And repeat until
The pieces can't fit anymore.

Your colours
Are psychedelics
To my eyes
Acid to my brain
You landed on
This thorny bush
And there's budding
In places I didn't know
Water could reach

Starlings

We watch a purple sky
With darting starlings
You ask what happened
To me finding myself
I smile, kiss your cheek

And say
"Don't be silly. Don't be silly."

I'm setting the mood,
tonight
With a jar full of fireflies
You will marvel at the moon
with her full belly
and cratered cheeks
I will lean in to get
you lost in the constellations
in my eyes

and I will wrap
my lips around you
and give
and take
and take
and take

I love you silly,
I love you clumsy,
I love you –
In the centre of the room
With my pants down and
Shoe laces tangled – embarrassing

So let the world laugh,
Let them gnaw away at my confidence
I've found love,
I've found love, damn it!

This is the kind of passion
Nations go to war for...
This is the kind of love
That gets gods crucified

You are for every season

In February, I stitch
My shadow to my ankle
To feel my own weight,
My own existence.
In March, I walk out
Of rooms with less love
And many more voices hissing
In my ears
My mirror screams "sand"
And I know that nothing will
Ever grow on this body
Flowers die here.
In April, I'm locked within walls
And my flesh gradually clings to my bones
My shadow comes loose
Then I become my own shadow
As the fabric of my existence
Frays.
In June, I hear a drop
On these sands
Who dares grow anything here?

In July, animals return to graze on
This skin
There's buzzing and footsteps
Around here again.
In July, it rained
And you made me drink from
The palm of your hands.
In August, you become
Time and creation
You become life, you become breathing
Go and tell everyone that
You feel different,
Run! Oh run!
This feels different!

You know,
Your last breath will save me
Tonight, or some other night
If I am to become a beautiful butterfly.
One day,
Your lips will be my diet,
My medicine.

Petrichor

The dust has started settling in my life
Since you came around
My heart, formerly a desert
Is bursting greens and yellows
Dancing birds and breeding nests
You have fallen hard on my misery
And left perfume and budding
Shrubs.

Dancer

Before the night ends,
Remind me to tell you of the time
You pointed my heart to where it
Always should be
Of the time I learned that my heart
Is a better dancer than I ever will be
That my body is more than just carbon
Atoms
A text, it was: "I'm madly in love with you, sir"
And knots came undone inside me.

Be grateful for the people
That walk into your life
And decide to stay
Knowing full well
That so much glass has been
Shattered here before

Butterfly, awake

I've found myself in spaces where
My body was covered in jeers
Where parts of me, I had to store away
Blank pages to keep from scarlet letters.
I know now what liberation feels like
That even when my tired muscles
Creak like old doors or mischief crawls
Under my skin
Or the stab wounds of being
Unwanted begin to bleed again
I am loved – if not in the flesh –
In thoughts and prayers
I am to be told "you are indeed beautiful"
I am to occupy spaces like a sweet fragrance
I am a boy who has crawled
A boy who lives now for flowers
And
Sunlight, and in many ways
An awakened butterfly.

Loic Ekinga Kalonji is a Congolese poet, storyteller, and a screenwriting enthusiast. His work in poetry and fiction focuses on the human experience and memories.

Loic has been featured in many online publications such as *Type/Cast Magazine*, *Ja. Magazine*, *Poetry Potion*, and *The Kalahari Review*. His experimental chapbook *Twelve Things You Failed at As A Man Today* was an honourable mention by JK Anowe for *Praxis Magazine Online*.

His short story 'Loop' has been adapted into a short film. He is a finalist of Poetry Africa's Slam Jam competition 2020. Loic currently resides in the south of Johannesburg where he reads, writes, and daydreams.